Spider Coloring Book

By Susan Potterfields

ISBN: 10: 1534819657
ISBN-13: 978-1534819658

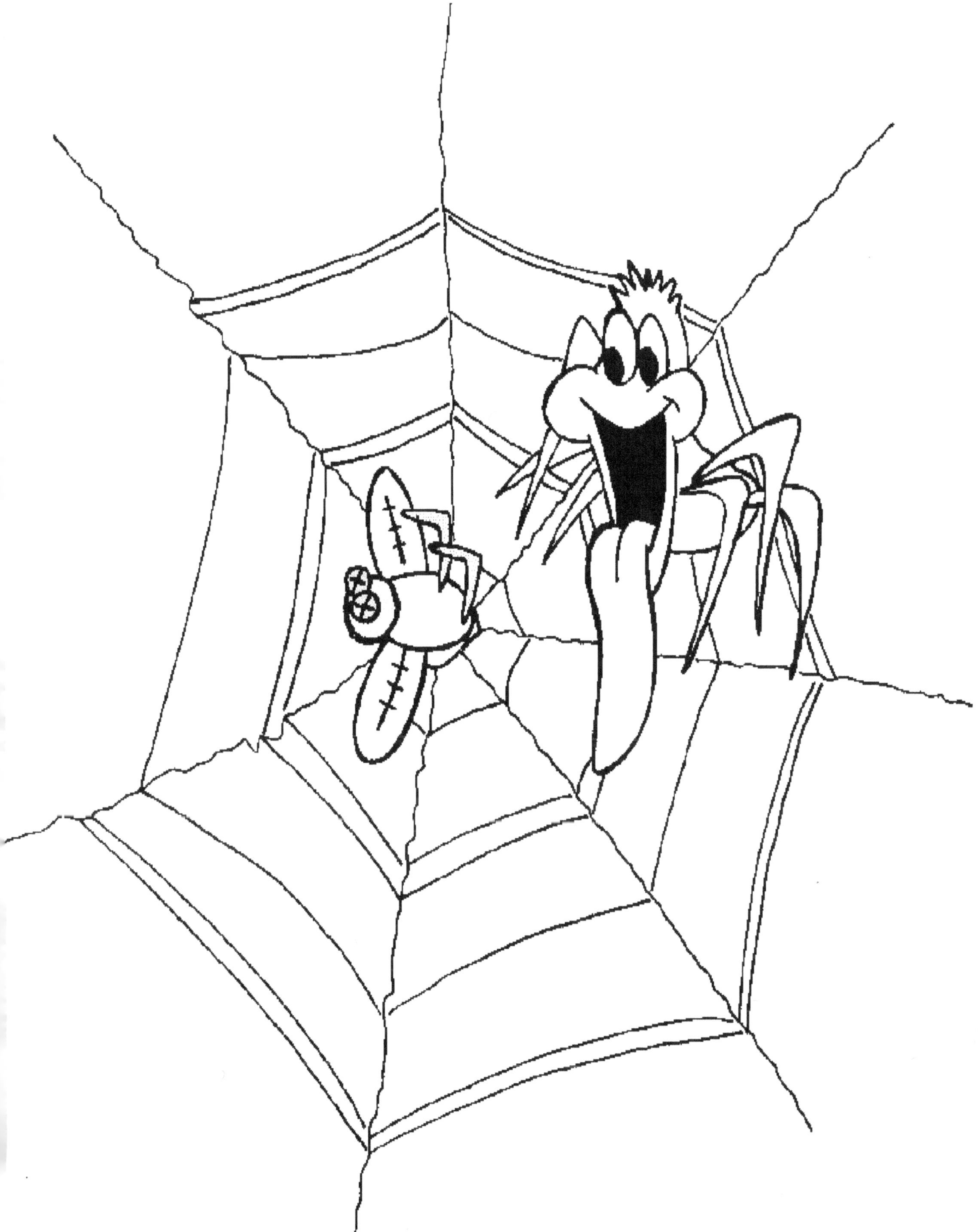

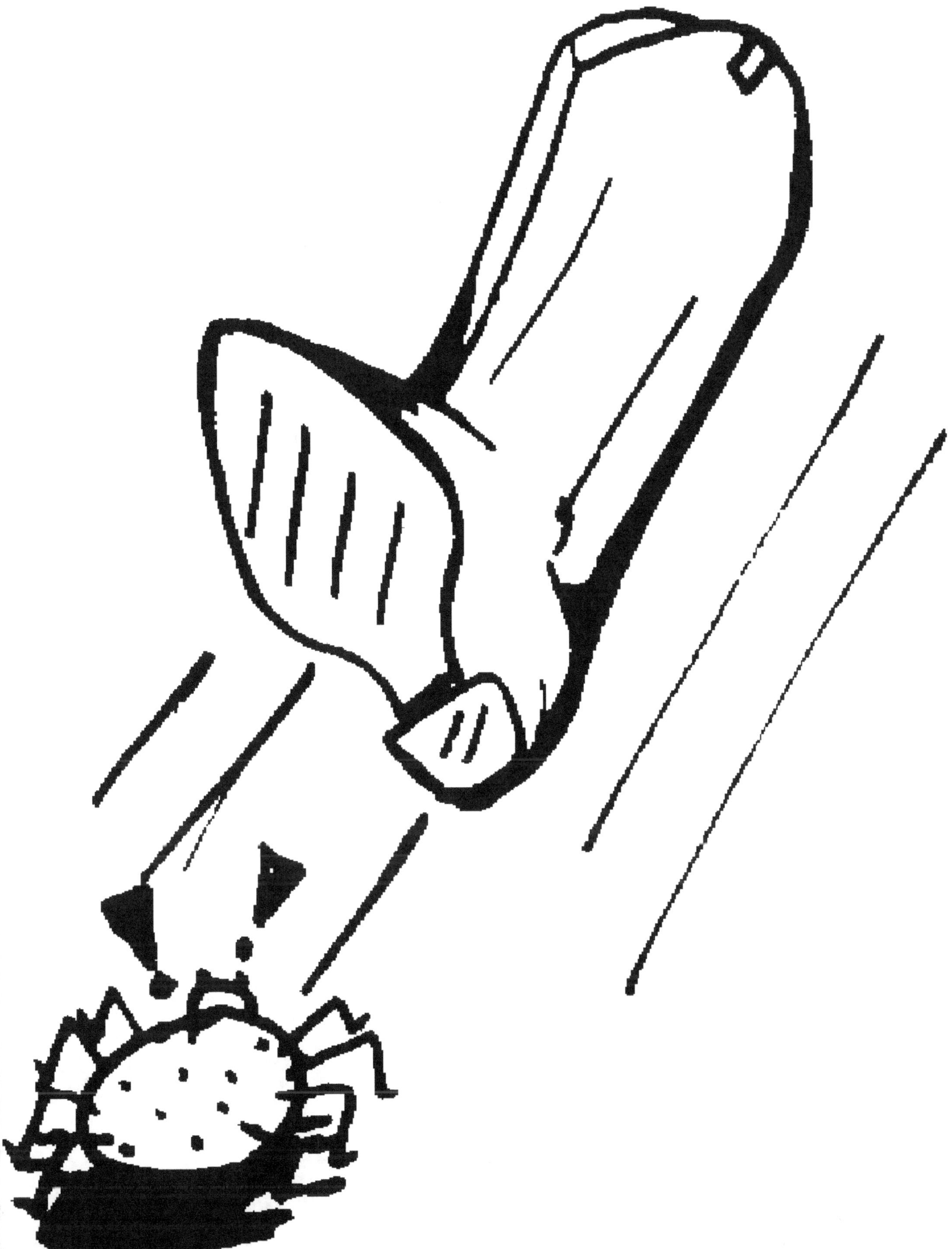

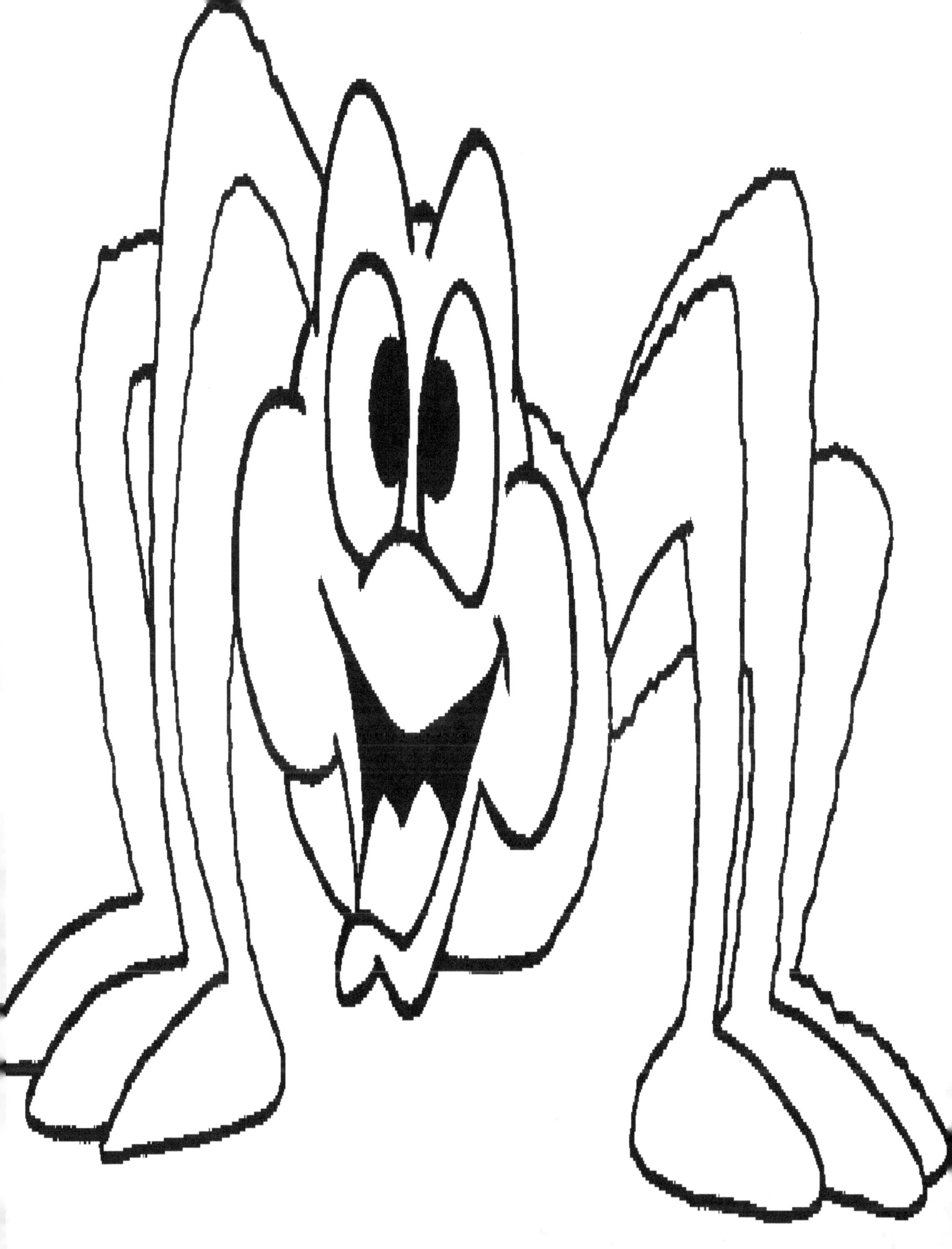

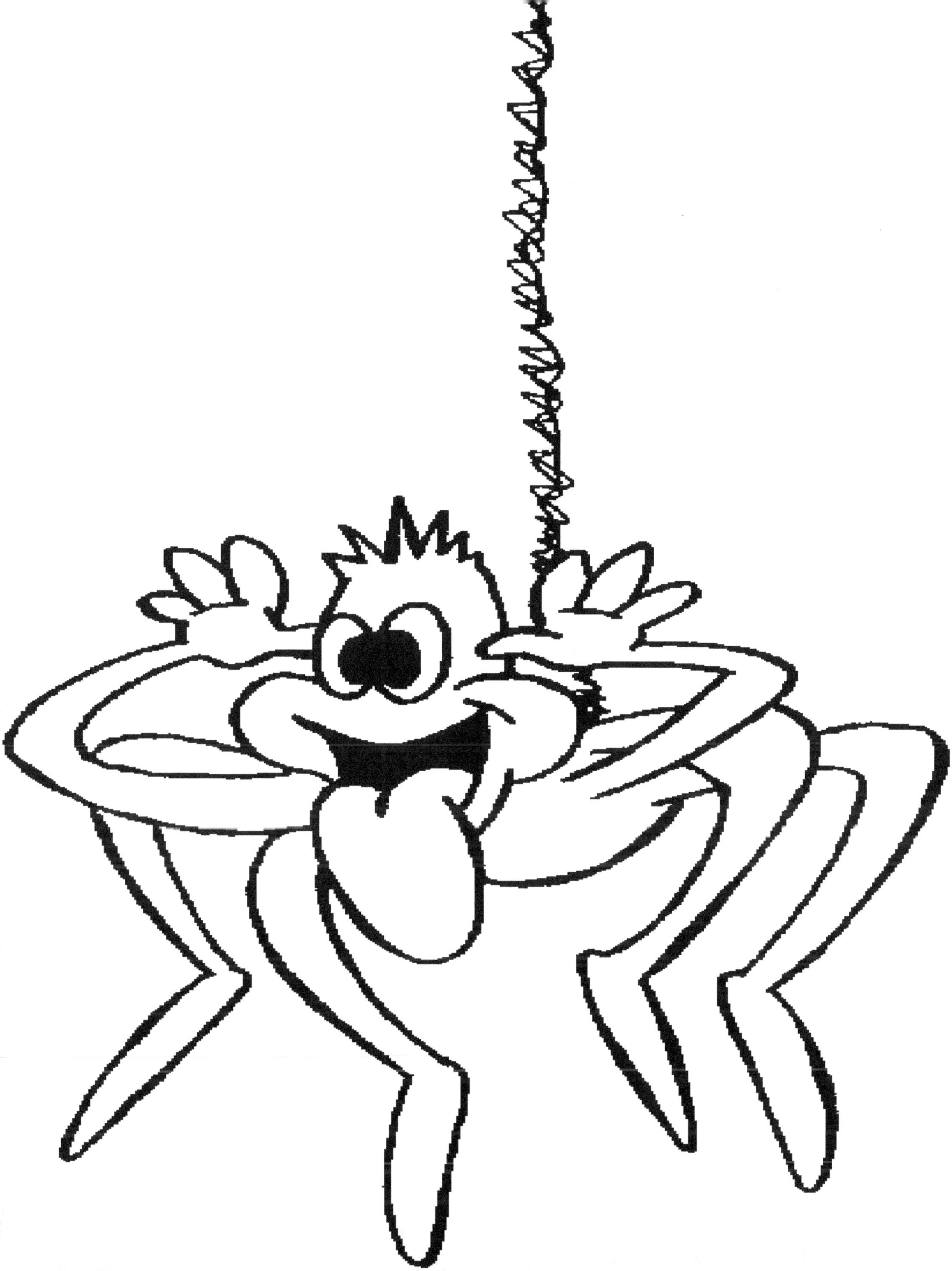

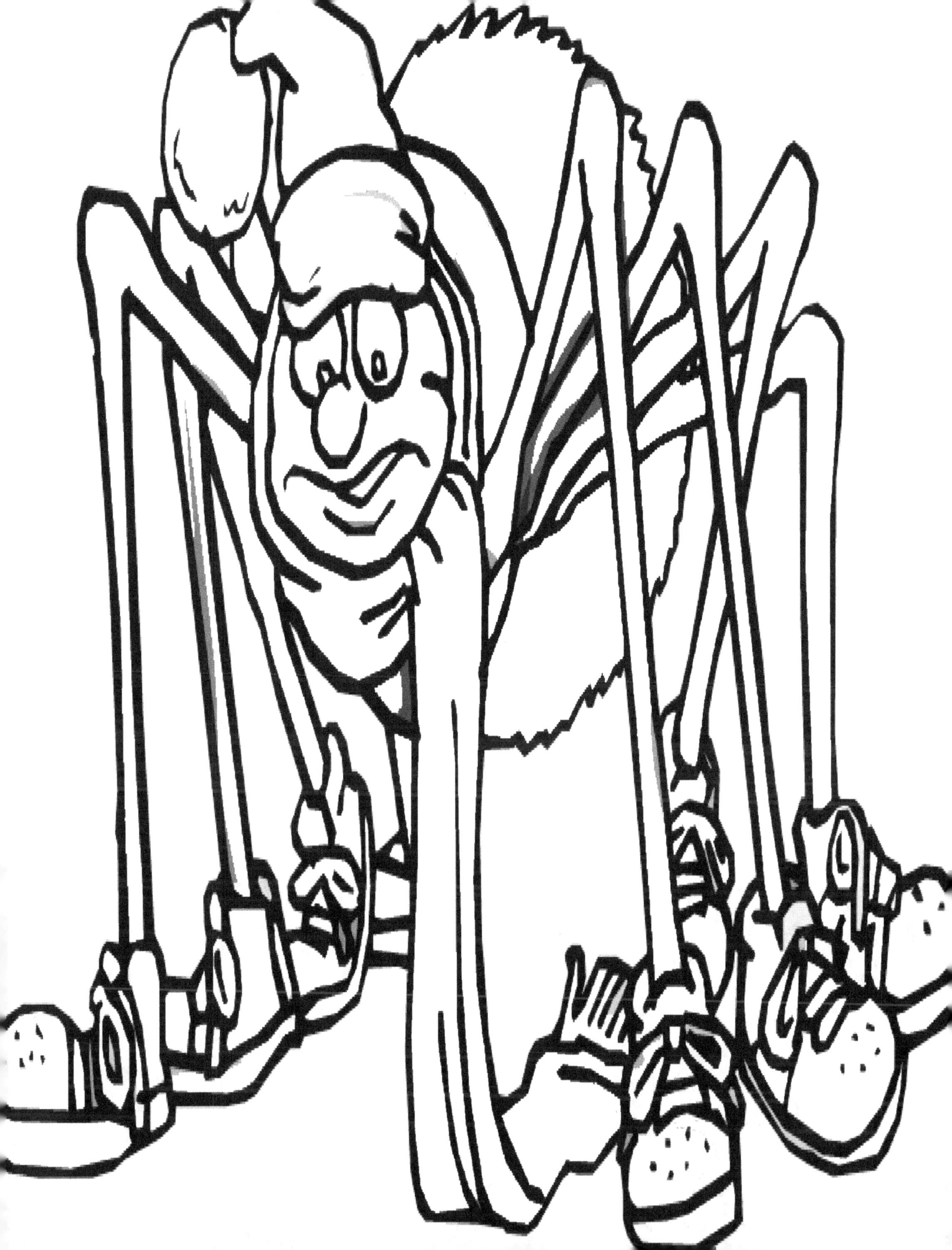

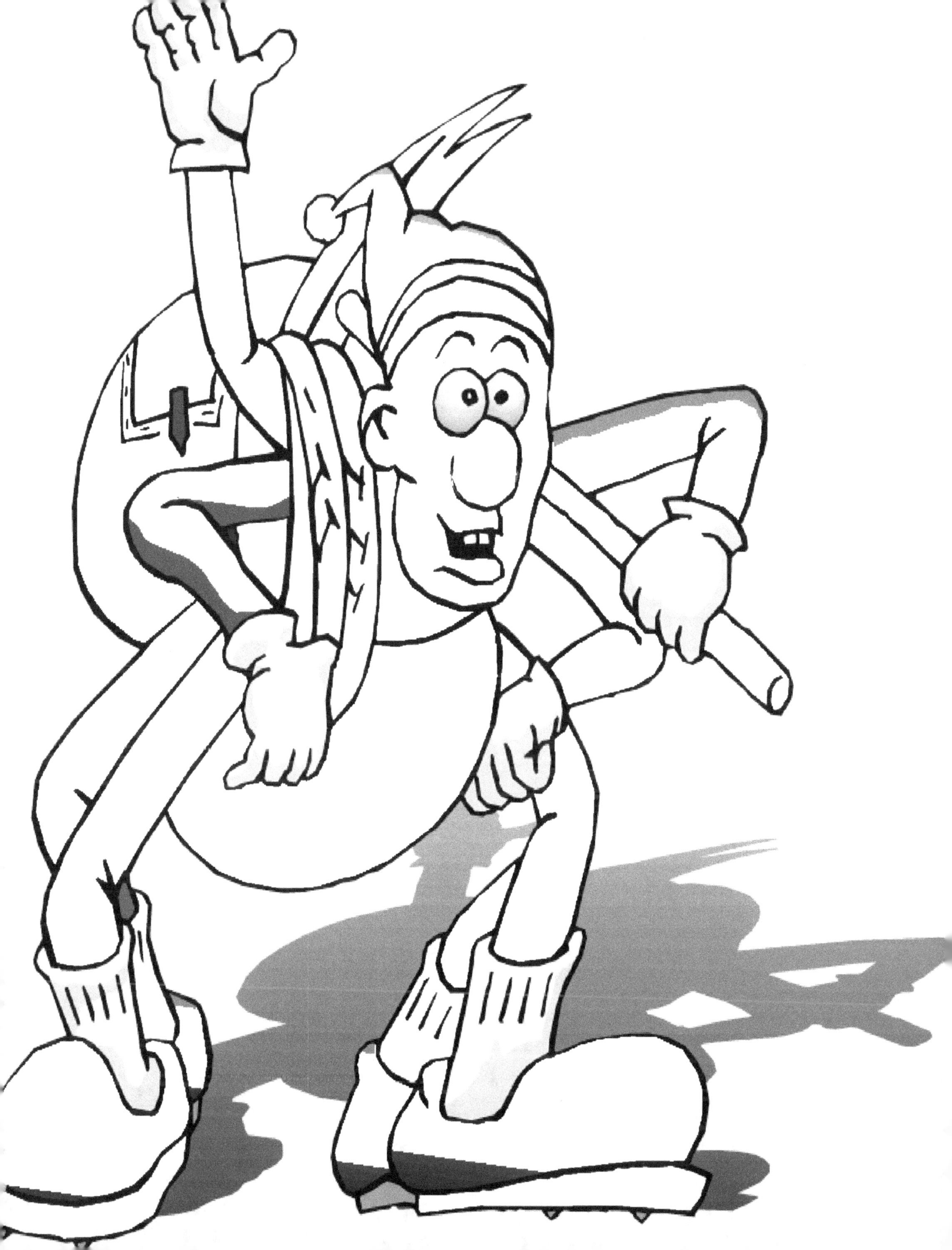

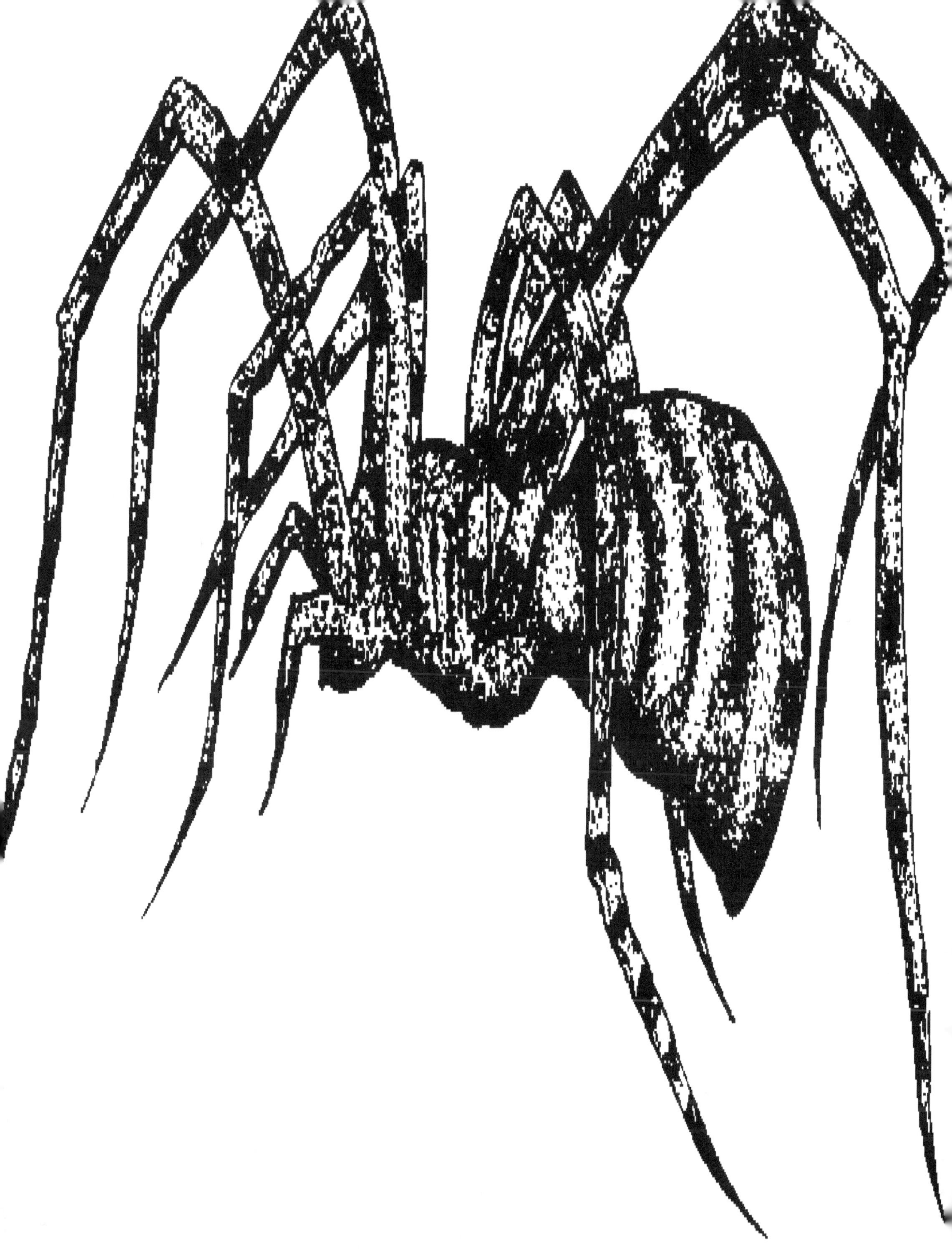

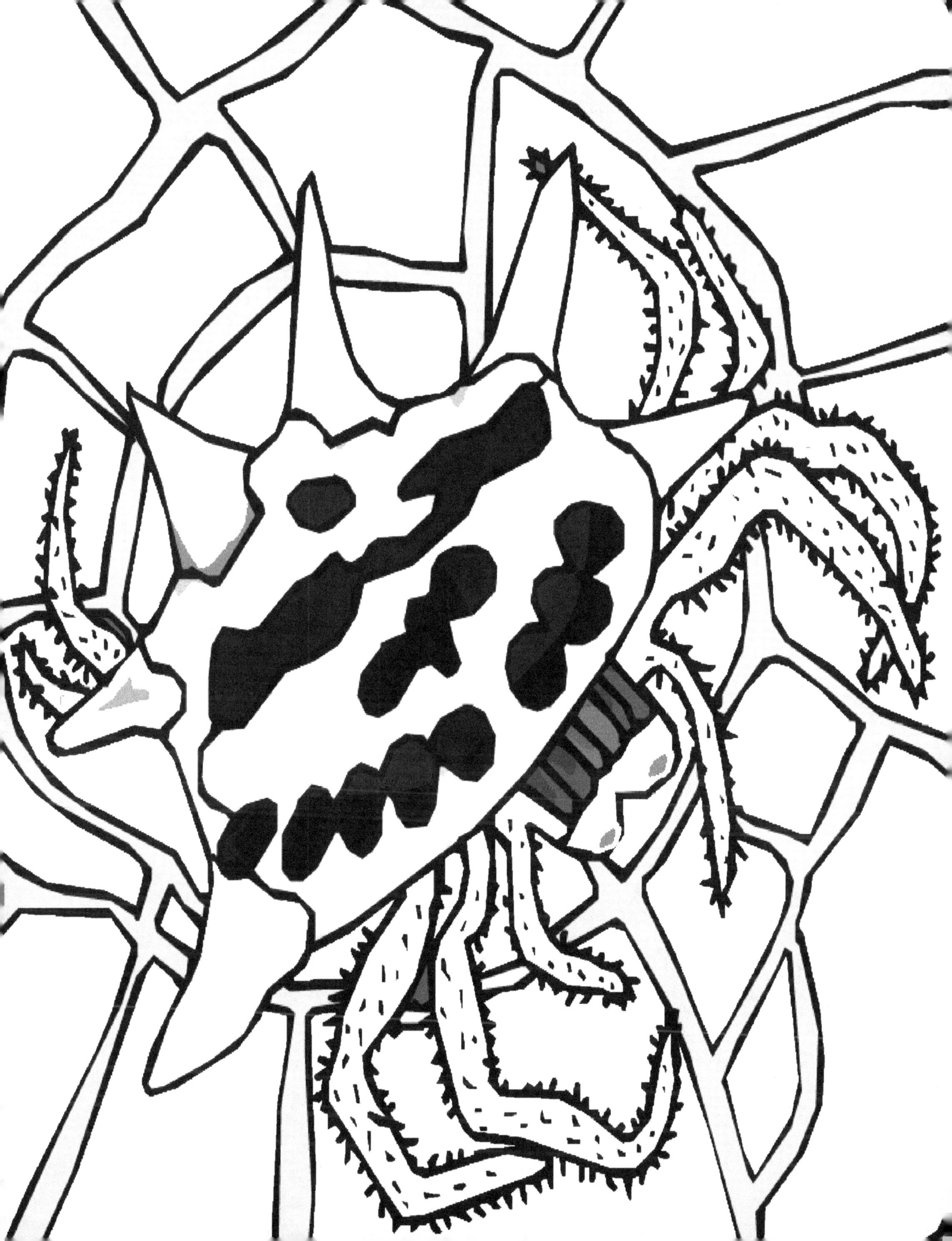

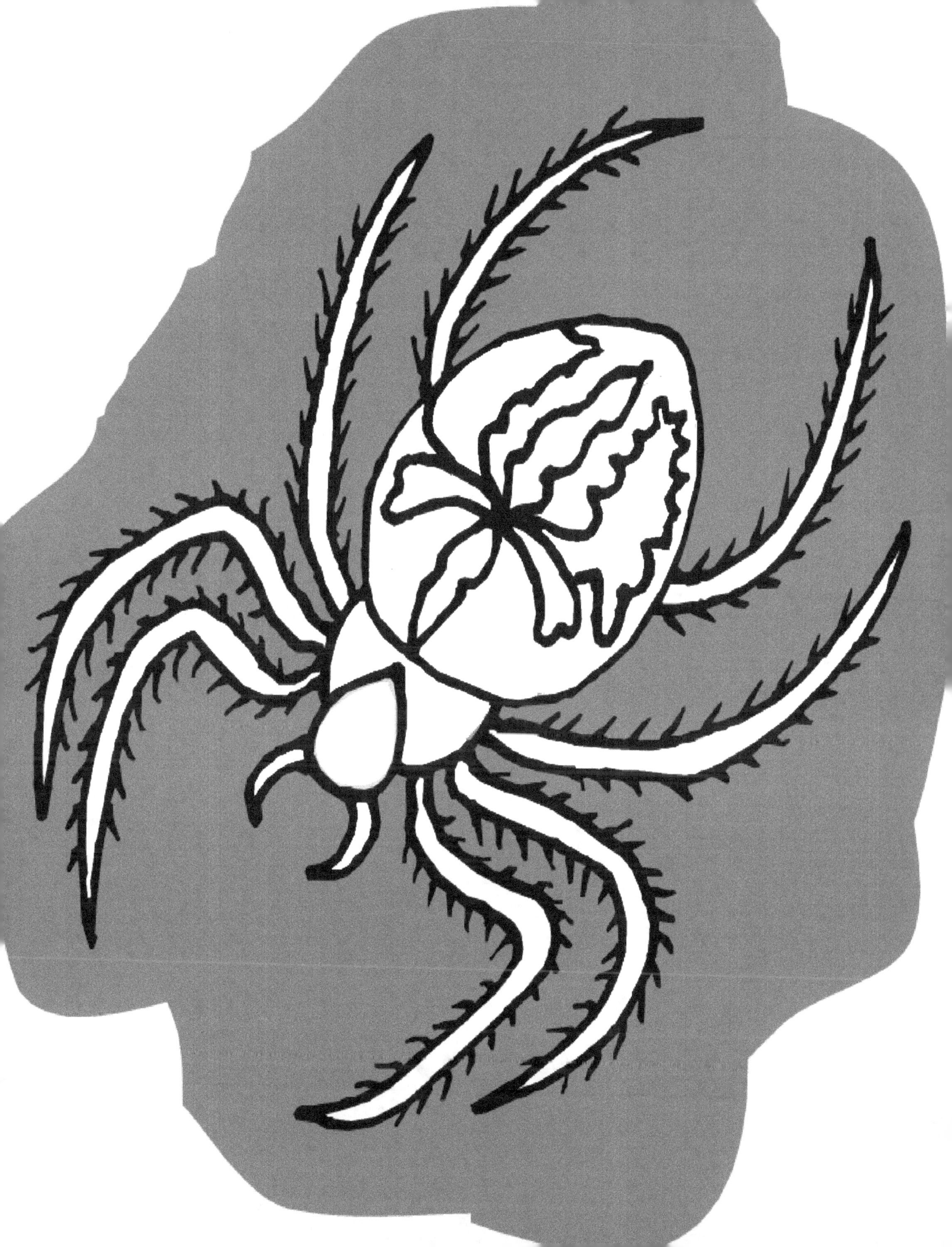

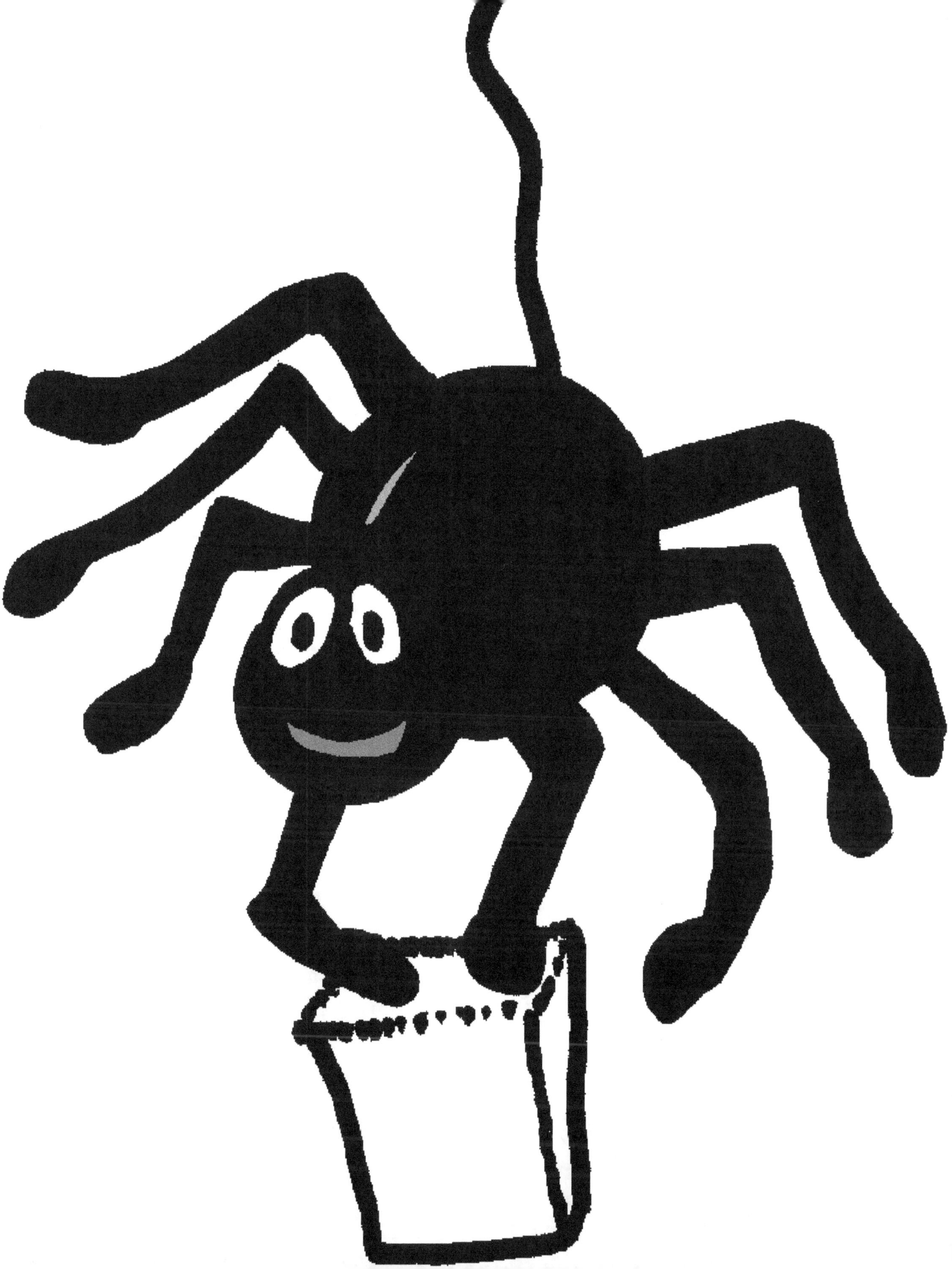

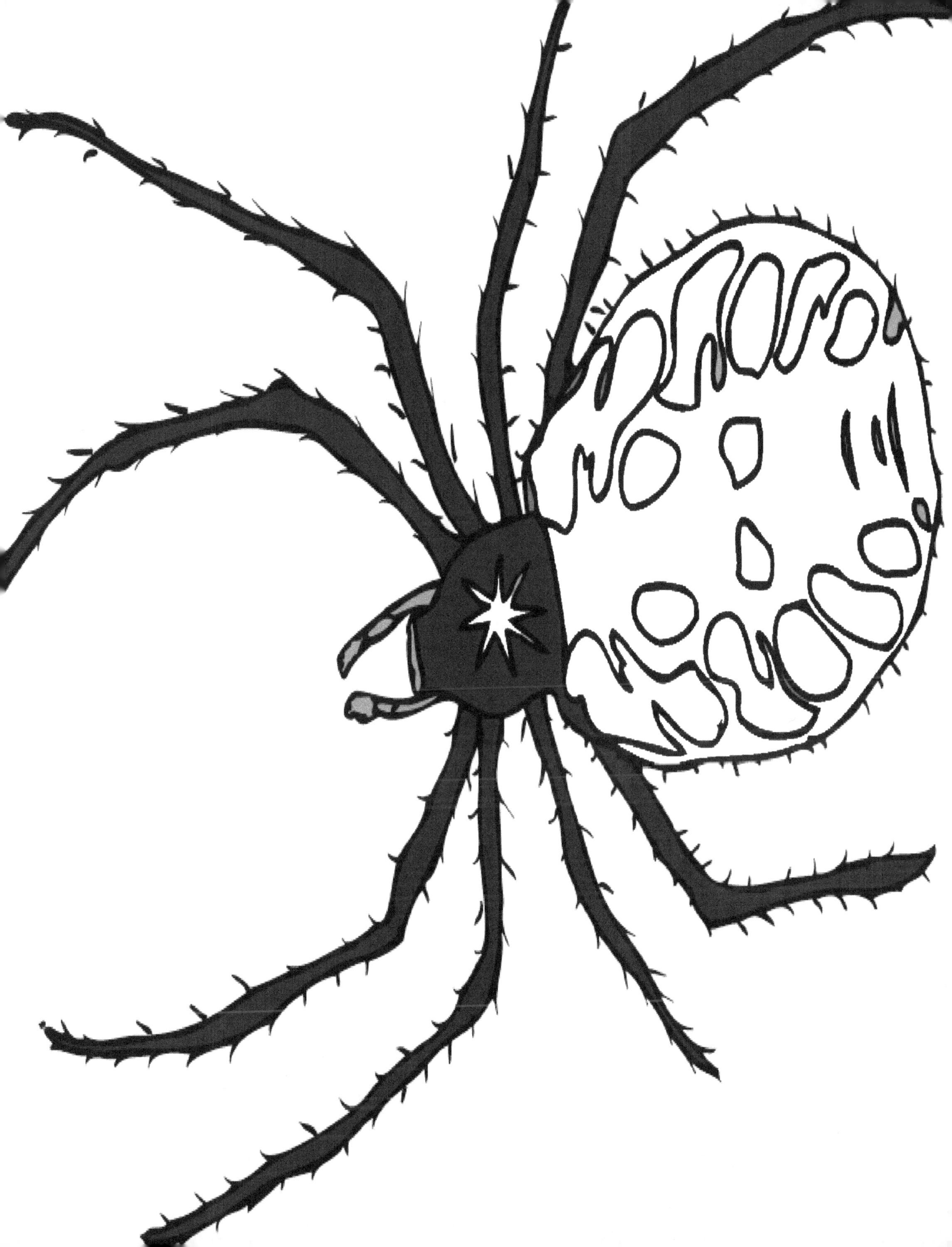

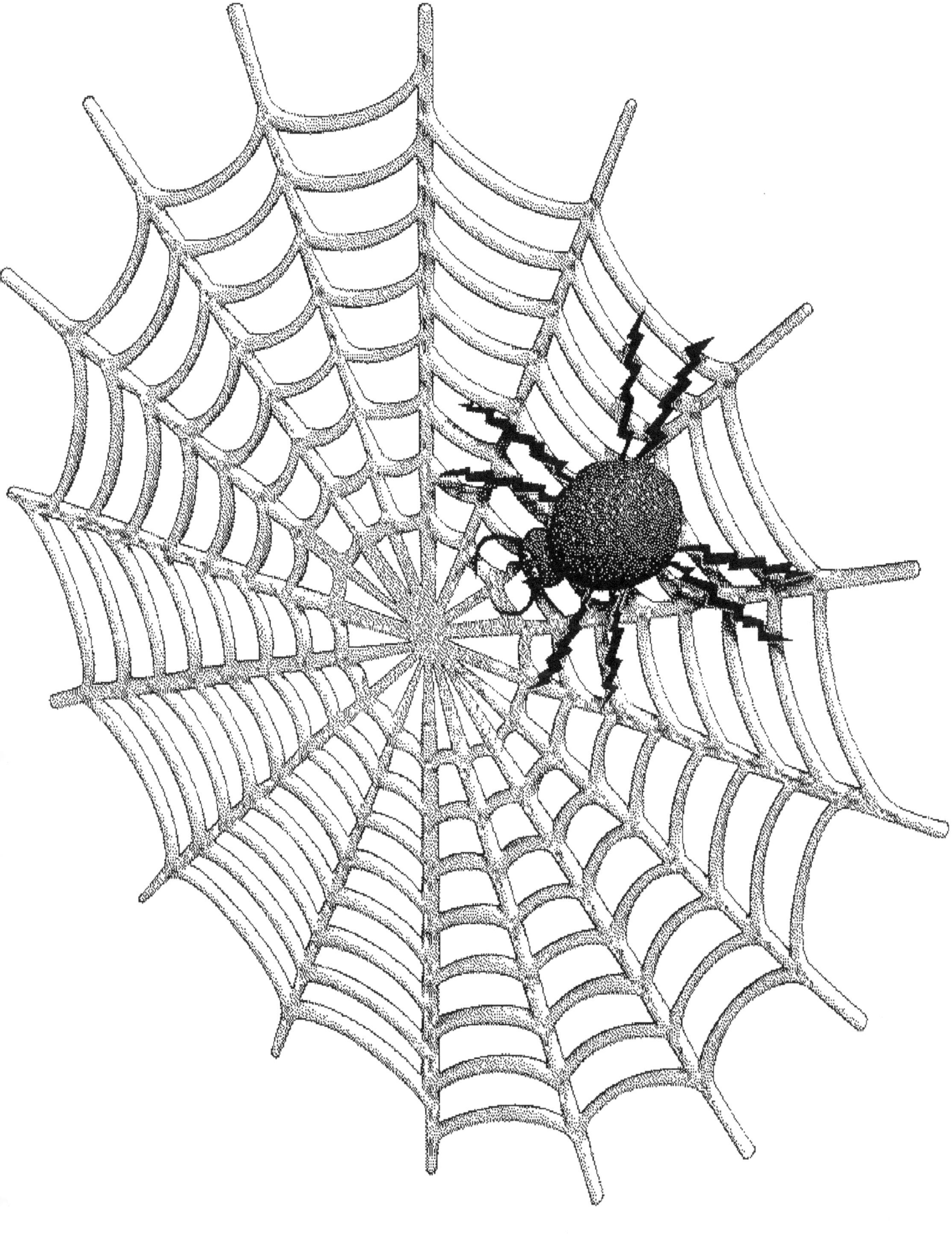

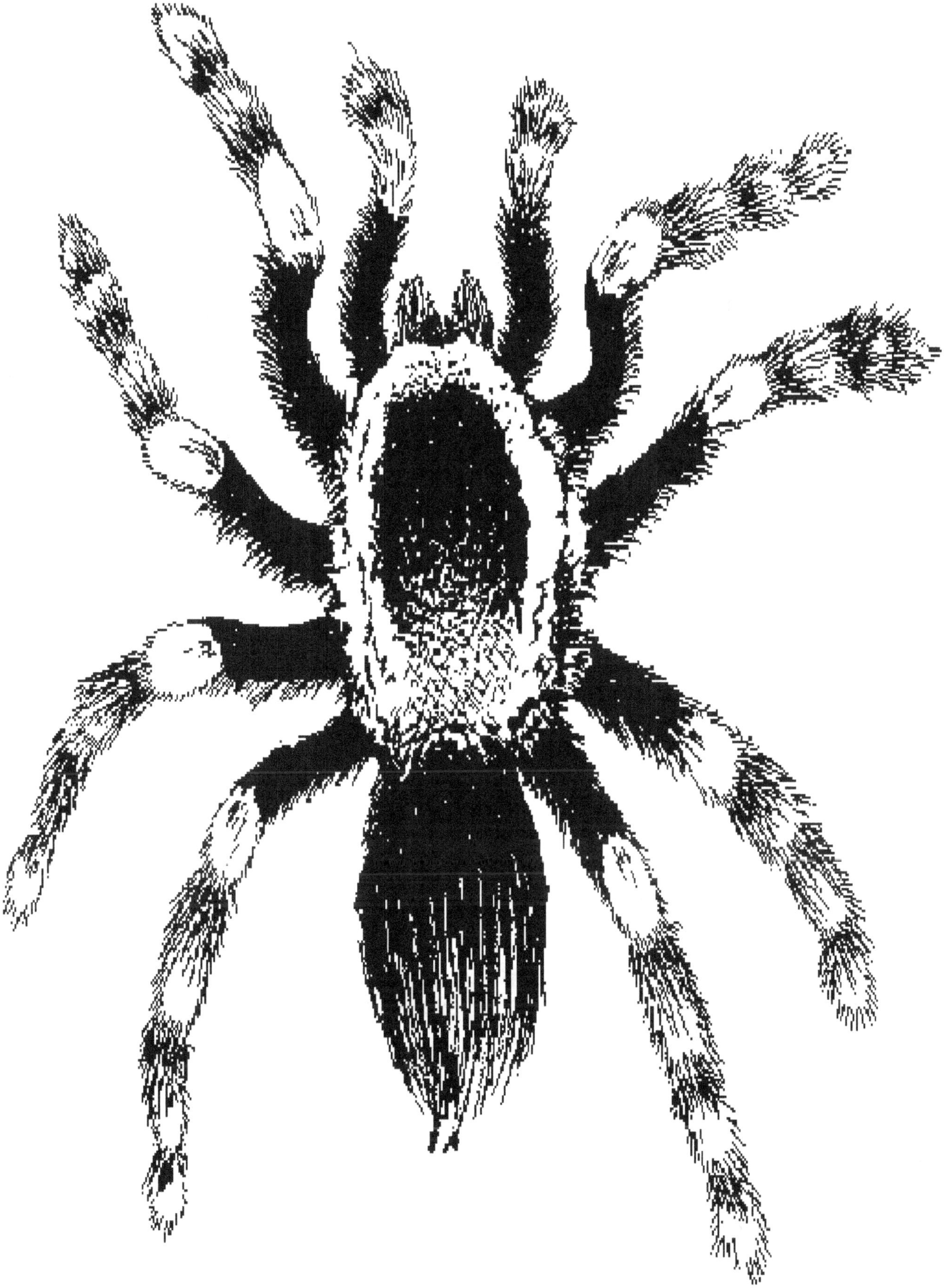

www.ingramcontent.com/pod-product-compliance
Lightning Source LLC
Chambersburg PA
CBHW081142280526
45787CB00007B/3187